LEARNING DISCUSSION SKILLS THROUGH GAMES

Gene Stanford
Director of Teacher Education Programs, Utica College of Syracuse University

Barbara Dodds Stanford
Assistant Professor of Education, Utica College of Syracuse University

CITATION PRESS   NEW YORK   1969

LB
1029
G3
57

3 3001 00669 5182

Library of Congress Catalog Card Number: 78-105863

Cover and line drawings by Stan Tusan

Copyright © 1969 by Scholastic Magazines, Inc. All rights reserved. Published by Citation Press, Professional Relations Division, Scholastic Magazines, Inc. Editorial office: 50 West 44th Street, New York, N. Y. 10036.

18 17 16 15 14 13 12 11 10 9 8 7   5 6 7 8 9/7 0/8

Printed in the U.S.A.

Introduction   7

Problems in Discussion   9

  Types of Discussion, 10
  Purposes of Discussion, 15
  How to Use this Book, 16

Skill-Building Sequence   18

  Skill 1: Getting Acquainted, 19
  Skill 2: Organizing for Action, 21
  Skill 3: Recognizing the Value of All Contributions, 23
  Skill 4: Taking Responsibility to Contribute, 31
  Skill 5: Responding to Other Contributions, 33
  Skill 6: Careful Listening to Perceive Differences, 36
  Skill 7: Careful Listening to Perceive Agreement, 38
  Skill 8: Encouraging Contribution Rather Than Argument, 39
  Skill 9: Learning New Roles, 41
  Skill 10: Arriving at a Consensus, 43

Remedial Exercises   50

   Problem 1: Obtaining Feedback, 51
   Problem 2: Group Polarized into Warring Factions, 56
   Problem 3: Hostile, Overly Aggressive Group, 60
   Problem 4: The Silent Group, 62
   Problem 5: Group Not Well Acquainted, 63
   Problem 6: Ignoring Contributions of Others, 64
   Problem 7: Dealing with Problem Members, 65
   Problem 8: Straying off the Topic, 67
   Problem 9: Fixed Patterns of Interaction, 68
   Problem 10: The Inhibited Group, 68
   Problem 11: Tossing Around Ideas Rather Than Building Group Product, 69
   Problem 12: Arguring without Agreed Definition, 70
   Problem 13: Illogical Reasoning, 71
   Problem 14: All Talking at Once, 72
   Problem 15: Low Trust Level, 72

On Your Own   74

About the Authors   76

INTRODUCTION

FOR A GROUP — whether it be a Boy Scout troop or a biology class — to work together well, its members must have certain basic skills. Willingness to work hard and a challenging goal are not, by themselves, enough to assure that the group will function effectively. Group members, for example, need to be aware of the importance of eliciting contributions from all members, not just the noisy few. They must be able to listen carefully to perceive areas of agreement and disagreement and to encourage contributions, rather than simply to pile more unrelated ideas onto the heap.

These are but a few of the skills necessary for being an effective group member. Yet most secondary students are not competent in these skills, and even fewer are conscious of their importance. Some students, particularly the brighter ones, may have developed the skills intuitively through experience. Most, however, need to be given the opportunity to learn and practice these basic skills before they can be expected to handle subject-matter discussions proficiently.

This book provides a sequence of skill-building games and activities designed to give students the necessary practice in proper discussion techniques; it also presents a repertoire of remedial devices for use whenever a group shows signs of a particular weakness in working together, such as all talking at once, extreme aggressiveness or hostility, or straying off the topic.

The structure of the games forces students to simulate an effective discussion, with emphasis on one particular skill at a time. The teacher can then help students apply what they have learned in playing the game to subject-matter discussions.

In testing these materials with our own students in an inner-city high school and a progressive suburban high school, we found that most students are sufficiently motivated by the entertaining nature of the games and that scoring and grading are therefore rarely necessary. It is possible, however, to grade students on many of the activities if the teacher feels it advisable. Primary emphasis, though, should be on the fact that the activities are interesting in themselves.

Our appreciation goes to Saville Sax of NEXTEP Associates, Southern Illinois University, Edwardsville, and to Aaron Hillman and George I. Brown of the Ford-Esalen Project in Affective Learning, who encouraged us in the use of games to improve communication and group relations.

GENE STANFORD
BARBARA DODDS STANFORD
August 1969

PROBLEMS IN DISCUSSION

"YOU DON'T KNOW nothing about nothing," shouted Nelson, half-rising from his seat and glaring menacingly toward Larry. "Your mother's a whore, and you ain't got no old man!"

Miss Jones, their well-meaning English teacher, interceded, "Since you refuse to discuss this topic intelligently, get out your grammar books and work the exercises on page forty-seven."

"I was expecting this," thought Miss Jones as she seated herself again. "It happens every time I try to let these low-average students discuss something."

Miss Jones' plight is shared by many teachers. She knows that students enjoy talking to one another. She sees them in the halls chatting enthusiastically about endless topics, but it seems that whenever she gives them an interesting topic to discuss in the classroom, they become either shy and withdrawn or noisily aggressive. We have all felt Miss Jones' frustration—have tried our best to devise fascinating discussion topics and appointed able student leaders, but achieved little or no success. Discussions seem to fall apart, or if not, to ramble on without attaining any sort of goal.

From the student's point of view, it is equally frustrating. He knows the teacher wants him to participate actively in a discussion; often his grade depends on it. Many times the topic is one that he is interested in and knows plenty about, yet he frequently finds himself failing to meet the teacher's expectations and having to face not only her ire but his own discomfort.

The authors themselves have experienced both kinds of frustration — first as students not really understanding what was expected of them in a discussion, and presently as high school teachers faced with structuring discussions. Convinced that students *can* be taught how to work together effectively, we devised the games and activities contained in this book for use with our own students. These activities are based on the premise that the ability to discuss effectively is a skill that can be taught to students and practiced by them. Not content to leave this learning process to chance, we have isolated the individual skills required for good discussion and have created or adapted activities that will provide proper practice in each.

TYPES OF DISCUSSION

One of the basic causes of a class's problems with discussions is that the teacher is not aware of the differences between the various types of discussion. Ask Miss Jones and her colleagues for an example of "a discussion," and their answers will range all the way from asking various students to name in order the kings of England to spending a half-hour imagining what would have happened if the South had won the Civil War.

Classroom discussions fall into four basic categories. The first is simple recitation. Serving the same function as testing, it enables the teacher to find out quickly what the student knows. It acts as an incentive to the student to do his lessons. It makes the student feel important for knowing the correct answers. It reviews the material for students and helps the teacher find areas that need more explanation. Recitation questions are fact questions and are either correct or incorrect. Usually one student answers a question asked by the teacher.

The second type of discussion is inductive questioning. Its purpose is usually to help students develop a concept. There is a "right" answer, and the teacher tries to lead students to it. Unlike recitation, inductive questioning does not test something the student already knows; rather it leads him to draw new conclusions from his information. The process requires careful organization by the teacher. Not only does the teacher set the goal, but he structures the steps leading toward attaining the goal. In teaching the concept of point of view in the short story, for example, a teacher may wish to use inductive questioning. He might arrange a group of objects on a table at the front of the room and have students describe what they see from various positions in the room. Building on this information, the teacher can ask a series of questions that will lead students to see that where the narrator stands in relation to the story determines his view of it.

Open-ended questions differ from recitation and inductive questioning in that the teacher asks a general question that has no right or wrong answers. Such a question might be, "Does the government have the right to force a person to sell his home to Negroes?" or "Was Brutus justified in killing Caesar?" Students state their opinions; they do not try to find the "right" answer. The purpose of this type of discussion is not to teach a concept but to encourage students to think and to value their own ideas as well as the ideas of others. The teacher functions only as a catalyst to keep the discussion going. Ideally in this type of nondirected discussion, students do not need to raise their hands; they share their ideas freely without being called on. The teacher usually does not respond to each student's contribution; rather he encourages other students to react to it.

The fourth type of discussion has solving a problem as its goal. The teacher sets the objective such as, "Design as a group a maximally safe automobile," or "Write a group composition with details arranged chronologically," or "Devise a fair solution to the Vietnam conflict." In this type of discussion there is a goal to be attained. Students must reach a consensus, not just share ideas. Ideas are pooled, but they must be integrated into a group product. The process differs from inductive questioning in that the answer has not been determined ahead of time by the teacher. The teacher may or may not serve as discussion leader. Students have freedom to produce their own answer or solution, and they themselves devise the steps leading to it.

The size and seating arrangement of a class should vary according to the type of discussion being used. In recitation and inductive questioning the teacher usually stands in front of a class of twenty to forty students. With open-ended questions and problem-solving, the class may work as one big unit in which approximately 25 students sit in one large circle with the teacher either outside the group or acting as a member of it. Usually, however, these latter two types of discussion are more effective when used with groups of five to twelve participants. In the conventional classroom setting this will require dividing the class into several smaller groups. In innovative programs the seminar is usually an ideal size. The need for students to see one another while they work together in problem-solving or answering open-ended questions makes it imperative that their desks be arranged in a circle. Sitting around a large table is perhaps even more effective, since most of us tend to feel "naked" when seated in a circle and prefer the security of a table to hide behind.

Just as the type of discussion dictates the size and arrangement of the group, the type of material and attitude of the teacher influence his selection of type of discussion. If the class is learning a body of facts needed as background data, the most effective method would probably be recitation. For concept learning, the teacher would probably select inductive questioning. If the teacher wishes students to examine their values and pool their opinions, he might rely on open-ended questions to spur nondirected discussion. If his purpose is to furnish students with an opportunity to synthesize and practice concepts they have already learned, the problem-solving approach would be effective.

The teacher should not assume that for each class period he must choose a single method of discussion. Rather, several methods can be used depending on the purposes of the teacher. Recitation, for example, is often a very effective way of beginning a class. The teacher obtains immediate feedback of what the students know and do not know, and students receive a quick review of the material they studied as homework. Then transition can be made to a less-directed form of discussion that allows students to share their ideas without trying to find the "right" answer. This process can also work in reverse. One of the authors, for instance, was sitting with a small group who were discussing some open-ended questions derived from the play *A Raisin in the Sun*. He noticed that the students were floundering because, as suburban whites, they had little understanding of the matriarchal structure of the Negro family. He stopped the group long enough to lead them to this concept through inductive questioning. They then proceeded with the nondirected discussion.

The attitude of the teacher can also determine which method of discussion he chooses to use. If he feels students are not intellectually capable of synthesizing and concept formation, he will limit his class discussions to recitation only. We feel, however, that all students are capable of synthesizing and concept formation. What seems to be a lack of intellectual ability is, we suspect, often inadequate skill in discussing.

A teacher might also choose recitation or inductive questioning if he feels afraid of giving up control of the class. Many of us have experienced the nerve-gripping fear that the class will go wild and start swinging from the light fixtures if we do not determine ahead of time exactly what they are going to accomplish and exactly what answers they must give to questions. This anxiety often springs from the good intentions of a teacher who has been taught in methods courses to be carefully prepared for every class. Yet deciding to allow students to grapple with a question that has no predetermined answer is not an indication of poor organization. It is the teacher's deliberate decision to simulate more closely the real world in which a person must use his own intellectual powers to deal with problems that do not always have a clearly defined solution.

Because of misconceptions such as these, teachers probably spend too much of their time in recitation and inductive questioning and not enough time with less directed forms of discussion. This may be because they have had groups that were not sufficiently skilled in nondirected discussion and these failures have left them frustrated and determined to structure classwork tightly. Or it may be that they are not really aware of the possibility of open-ended questions and the problem-solving discussion. Therefore in this book emphasis is placed on these latter two types. Most teachers are already competent at leading recitation — perhaps that's the form of discussion they were most often subjected to as students. Inductive questioning requires a considerable amount of skill on the part of the teacher, but anyone who is eager to develop these skills can find several good books on the subject. But the teacher who wants to use open-ended questions and problem-solving and finds himself with an unskilled group of students, has few sources of help for training his students to discuss more effectively.

This book was developed to provide that help. It furnishes the means through which teachers can train their students to participate more effectively in discussions that are generally not teacher-directed and in which either the goals or the means toward the goals are not specified explicitly by the teacher.

PURPOSES OF DISCUSSION

These types of discussions have several purposes: to solve problems, to air opinions, to find out what others think, to vent feelings, to clarify one's point of view, to re-evaluate one's opinions, and to gain feelings of acceptance and belonging. Not every nondirected discussion will serve all these purposes, but a good discussion will satisfy at least some of them.

Ironically, however, discussions too often produce just the opposite effects. Participants may withhold their true opinions, avoid expressing their honest feelings, fail to examine their own views, adhere even more tightly to their unexamined values and ideas, and feel defensive and uncomfortable. In a typical class discussion some students become angry and begin ridiculing those who hold differing views. As a result, many of the other students withdraw and keep their opinions to themselves. Others become excited by the heat of battle and vehemently support any opinion that will allow them to enter the fray. In the worst instances, all members leave the discussion entrenched in their unexamined opinions and convinced that the other members hate them.

A good discussion should take place in a climate that encourages all persons to share their ideas openly and without fear of embarrassment. It should encourage them to work together, rather than splitting into warring camps or isolating themselves as individuals. A good discussion leads toward a group product that is better than any individual working alone could produce. It encourages participants to re-examine their own feelings and ideas and change them without fear of losing face. And it encourages them to listen carefully and in depth to what others are saying.

A discussion meeting these criteria can result when students are sufficiently skilled in the techniques of discussion. But teaching students these skills requires more than telling them how groups best work together. Merely outlining on the blackboard the steps involved in good discussion and then expecting students to do well is as foolish as telling a medical student how to perform brain surgery and expecting him to be successful. Students need to practice the individual skills that are required in good discussion. They must see what form a good discussion takes. For this reason, we have designed games and activities that force students into proper patterns of interaction. Students and teacher can then discuss the results and attempt transferring the skills to subject-matter discussions. By their nature the games heighten motivation and make practicing the skills more enjoyable than if the teacher simply harped at the students about their ineffective work.

HOW TO USE THIS BOOK

The activities and games presented here can be adapted for use in any of the secondary grades, and some could even be used on the elementary level. The teacher can easily make such adaptations as he feels necessary.

The second chapter consists of a basic sequence of games designed to teach the skills essential for effective discussion. It is probably best used whenever a group comes together for the first time, but it can be used at any time with any group, no matter how long they have been working together. This sequence begins with the most basic element of discussion — finding out who the other group members are — and proceeds systematically, developing one skill at a time and building on skills learned previously. Most of the activities do not require an entire period, and many can be used in conjunction with subject-matter goals. Therefore, using the complete sequence at the beginning of a term would not preclude doing some subject-matter work during the time that emphasis is being given to developing discussion skills.

The teacher who wishes to use this sequence should study the entire series carefully and incorporate the games and activities into his lesson plans for a two-week period. He should familiarize himself with not only the instructions for playing the games but also the rationale underlying the design of the activities and the possible ways of following up the games with appropriate discussions of what was learned.

The third chapter consists of single games and activities useful for teaching more advanced skills or for remedying problems that the group may encounter at later stages. These can be viewed by the teacher as prescriptions for the ills he may diagnose in his class's discussion work. To use these games most effectively, the teacher must have internalized them thoroughly so that he can call them up at a moment's notice whenever the problems arise. In other words, knowledge of these activities will give the teacher a repertory of remedial exercises to use whenever a group demonstrates a particular weakness.

SKILL-BUILDING SEQUENCE

THE DEVELOPMENTAL SEQUENCE of discussion activities outlined in the following pages can help the teacher structure a program of concentrated instruction and practice in discussion skills. When used at the beginning of a school term, it will enable a teacher to proceed with subject-matter discussions with the knowledge that his students possess adequate discussion ability. When used as a crash program in the middle of a term, at the point when a teacher comes to the undeniable realization that his students simply don't know how to work together, it will provide much-needed rehabilitation for the ailing group. Under both sets of circumstances, the sequence should be followed in the order outlined here, since later activities build on skills developed in earlier ones. An eager group can gallop through the sequence in two weeks, or a teacher can choose to follow the sequence at a more leisurely pace, interspersing the activities with other lessons and allowing time for additional practice of each skill in actual classroom activities before moving on to a new skill.

The sequence consists of games and activities to develop proficiency in each of ten individual discussion skills. We have explained how weaknesses in each skill will affect classroom discussion and how the practice provided by the game or activity will help overcome the weakness. Instructions for directing the playing of the games are given, followed by possible variations. Finally, we have furnished suggestions for how the teacher can inductively lead students, after playing the game, to verbalize what they have learned and to transfer the skill to subject-matter discussions.

SKILL 1: GETTING ACQUAINTED

In our how-to-do-it education courses, all of us were taught the importance of a teacher's learning students' names quickly at the beginning of the term. Of equal importance is that students come to know one another quickly. Not only should they learn which name goes with which face, but they need to start piecing together information as to what kind of people these other group members are. Therefore, introductions should be the first order of business. Since students are just as uncomfortable in this process as we are in a similar situation (just remember the last time a substitute appeared in the faculty lounge, and you had to nudge yourself into saying simply, "Hello, I'm Roberta Johnson; I'm in the math department."), a structured framework for making introductions is helpful. If everyone has to introduce himself in a routine way, the discomfort seems to be less. In addition to telling their names, students should be encouraged to provide information about themselves that will help others know them better. Students should also be urged to formulate from this information a first impression of the other members of the group.

Game

Chairs are arranged in a semi-circle so that all students can see one another. The teacher sits with students in the circle.

Each group member, starting with the teacher, goes to the blackboard, writes his name clearly, tells the group his name, and describes himself. The choice of information to be revealed is left up to each member but might include such things as hobbies, after-school activities, interests, likes, dislikes, and so forth. After all students have introduced themselves, conduct a contest to see who can remember the most names. In a large group it might be easier to have students try writing down the names in order around the circle and see who has the longest, most accurate list. Or anyone who wishes to compete might go around the circle, naming the names orally until he misses; then some other student can try, and so on until someone is able to name all names correctly.

After students have become fairly familiar with each others' names, encourage them to verbalize their first impressions of each other. In a small, apparently friendly group this might be done orally by going around the circle "telling what you now know about each person in the group." Perhaps it would be less threatening for each student to make a written record of his first impression of all the others. These could be collected by the teacher and saved for a day later in the term when they would be given back to the students who wrote them and perhaps shared with the group.

Second Try

Each student — as though he were a visiting celebrity — is interviewed by a panel of "reporters" appointed by the teacher. The interviewers ask questions about the "celebrity" to elicit information that they think all members of the group would like to know. The "celebrity" has the right not to answer any questions that make him uncomfortable. The process continues until all group members have been interviewed, with the teacher appointing a new panel of "reporters" from time to time. Then all students can write down or discuss their first impressions of each "celebrity" as outlined above.

SKILL 2: ORGANIZING FOR ACTION

Maintaining order within a group is a basic skill that needs constant attention and reinforcement. Students must learn why they cannot all talk at once, and they need to develop possible ways to control this tendency. In some cases agreeing on a chairman or sergeant-at-arms to maintain order is the only hope. In other groups self-discipline and simple courtesy will suffice. But group members themselves should decide how much control they need and how they wish to organize to provide it. In the game below students are given a simple task to perform — one that involves every member to at least some degree — and are turned loose to perform it. The teacher should not interfere with suggestions on how to organize the group, so that members themselves will realize inductively — though probably after a great deal of chaos — that control and organization are necessary.

Game

Students are seated in a circle with the teacher standing outside the group. *Only* the following directions are to be given:

> You are to calculate the average height in feet and inches of the members of this group. If a member does not know his exact height, he may give an estimate. The group must agree on the answer and appoint someone to submit it to the teacher.

Repeat directions until all students understand them. Then step away and do not talk to the group until the problem is solved.

Follow-Up

Careful discussion of the process used for solving the problem will help students understand possible ways of organizing a group. Focus discussion on questions such as:

What slowed the group down?
What problems did it have in organizing?
Did anyone take over leadership?
Is this good or bad?
Was a leader needed?
What responsibility did each member have?
How could the group solve the problem faster next time?

Second Try

If the group is having serious difficulty organizing itself, a teacher may wish to repeat this game several times. Variations might include calculating the average weight of the members, solving a riddle (*Reader's Digest* often has useful puzzles of this type), or answering a subject-matter question.

SKILL 3: RECOGNIZING THE VALUE OF ALL CONTRIBUTIONS

Every teacher has struggled with the problem of the group that ignores some of the members. Frequently more aggressive students will monopolize the discussion but accomplish little more than wheel spinning, since they have limited information they can bring to bear on the problem. The more timid group members will often quietly acquiesce, happy for someone else to carry the burden of the discussion or resentful that they are not being included. Group members need to learn that in trying to arrive at an answer to a question they must elicit contributions from every member and consider all contributions carefully. The vocal members must avoid stifling the timid ones by showing off their knowledge, and the quieter members must recognize their responsibility to share their ideas with the group.

The following activity demonstrates to students the need for considering the information every group member can contribute and gives them practice in organizing to accomplish the task. Every member is given an essential piece of information — a clue in a murder mystery — so that no student can excuse himself from participation on the grounds that he "doesn't know anything about the topic." In addition to forcing the group to consider every piece of information, the game will reinforce the group's previous learning of ways to organize for problem solving (Skill 2).

Game

Students are seated in a circle with the teacher standing outside the group. The teacher gives the following explanation:

> Today we are going to play another game that will help improve your discussion skills. Each of the pieces of paper I am holding contains one clue that

will help you solve a murder mystery. If you put all the facts together, you will be able to solve the mystery. You must find the *murderer,* the *weapon,* the *time* of the murder, the *place* of the murder, and the *motive.* Any time you think you know the answers and the group agrees on the guess, you may tell me. I will only tell you whether all five answers are right or wrong. If part of your answers are incorrect, I will not tell you which answers are wrong.

You may organize yourselves in any way you like. You may not, however, pass your clues around or show them to anyone else, and you may not leave your seats to walk around the group. All sharing of clues and ideas must be done verbally.

After clarifying the rules, pass out the clues. If there are more than 27 students, make up extra clues or have some students share clues. Some students should be appointed to serve as observers and timekeepers. The observers can make suggestions about how the group could be better organized and work faster. The teacher stands unobtrusively in the background, indicating the passing of time on the blackboard. He should not interrupt, make suggestions, or give hints.

Following are the clues, all of which are needed to solve the mystery. Type them (making several carbon copies for future use) on sheets of paper, leaving plenty of space between clues for cutting them apart.

When he was discovered dead, Mr. Kelley had a bullet hole in his thigh and a knife wound in his back.

Mr. Jones shot at an intruder in his apartment building at 12:00 midnight.

The elevator operator reported to police that he saw Mr. Kelley at 12:15 a.m.

The bullet taken from Mr. Kelley's thigh matched the gun owned by Mr. Jones.

Only one bullet had been fired from Mr. Jones' gun.

When the elevator man saw Mr. Kelley, Mr. Kelley was bleeding slightly, but he did not seem too badly hurt.

A knife with Mr. Kelley's blood on it was found in Miss Smith's yard.

The knife found in Miss Smith's yard had Mr. Scott's fingerprints on it.

Mr. Kelley had destroyed Mr. Jones' business by stealing all his customers.

The elevator man saw Mr. Kelley's wife go to Mr. Scott's apartment at 11:30 p.m.

The elevator operator said that Mr. Kelley's wife frequently left the building with Mr. Scott.

Mr. Kelley's body was found in the park.

Mr. Kelley's body was found at 1:30 a.m.

Mr. Kelley had been dead for one hour when his body was found, according to a medical expert working with police.

The elevator man saw Mr. Kelley go to Mr. Scott's room at 12:25 a.m.

The elevator man went off duty at 12:30 a.m.

It was obvious from the condition of Mr. Kelley's body that it has been dragged a long distance.

Miss Smith saw Mr. Kelley go to Mr. Jones' apartment building at 11:55 p.m.

Mr. Kelley's wife disappeared after the murder.

Police were unable to locate Mr. Scott after the murder.

When police tried to locate Mr. Jones after the murder, they discovered that he had disappeared.

The elevator man said that Miss Smith was in the lobby of the apartment building when he went off duty.

Miss Smith often followed Mr. Kelley.

Mr. Jones had told Mr. Kelley that he was going to kill him.

Miss Smith said that nobody left the apartment building between 12:25 a.m. and 12:45 a.m.

Mr. Kelley's blood stains were found in Mr. Scott's car.

Mr. Kelley's blood stains were found on the carpet in the hall outside Mr. Jones' apartment.

ANSWER: After receiving a superficial gunshot wound from Mr. Jones, Mr. Kelley went to *Mr. Scott's apartment* where he was killed by *Mr. Scott* with a *knife* at *12:30 a.m.* because *Mr. Scott was in love with Mr. Kelley's wife.*

Follow-Up

Help student to understand what caused the problems the group had in solving the mystery. If they were relatively successful in completing the work quickly, discuss the reasons

for their success. Questions should focus first on the skills learned earlier:

> Was a leader needed?
> How was time lost in getting organized?
> Why was it ineffective for everyone to try to talk at once?

Finally students should discuss the need for the group to encourage everyone to contribute and to consider the contributions carefully:

> What problems arose because some people didn't present their clues?
> What should they have done?
> In what ways did some members ignore the clues of others?
> Was any attempt made to urge all persons to present their clues?
> Did anyone ever forget a clue and make an incorrect inference?
> Were all members included in solving the problem?
> Did anyone monopolize the discussion?

Second Try

If the group scored poorly on this exercise, they may plead for another chance. Below are the clues for another mystery, this time a bank robbery. The First National Bank of Minnetonka, Minnesota, was robbed of $1,000,000. Students are to discover what *person(s)* did it. Instructions can be given in the same form as above. Follow-up discussion can be based on the questions suggested above.

> The robbery was discovered at 8:00 a.m. on Friday, November 12. The bank had closed at 5:00 p.m. the previous day.
>
> Miss Margaret Ellington, a teller at the bank, discovered the robbery.
>
> The vault of the bank had been blasted open by dynamite.
>
> The president of the bank, Mr. Albert Greenbags, left before the robbery was discovered. He was arrested by authorities at the Mexico City airport at noon on Friday, November 12.
>
> The president of the bank had been having trouble with his wife, who spent all of his money. He had frequently talked of leaving her.
>
> The front door of the bank had been opened with a key.
>
> The only keys to the bank were held by the janitor and the president of the bank.
>
> Miss Ellington often borrowed the president's key to open the bank early when she had an extra amount of work to do.

A strange, hippie-type person had been hanging around the bank on Thursday, November 11, watching employees and customers.

A substantial amount of dynamite had been stolen from the Acme Construction Company on Wednesday, November 10.

An Acme employee, Howard Ellington, said that a hippie had been hanging around the construction company on Wednesday afternoon.

The hippie-type character, whose name was Dirsey Flowers and who had recently dropped out of Southwest Arkansas State Teachers College, was found by police in East Birdwatch, about ten miles from Minnetonka.

Dirsey Flowers was carrying $500 when police apprehended him and had thrown a package into the river as the police approached.

Anastasia Wallflower of East Birdwatch, Wisconsin, said that she had bought $500 worth of genuine Indian love beads from Dirsey Flowers for resale in her boutique in downtown East Birdwatch.

Anastasia said that Dirsey had spent the night of November 11th at the home of her parents and left after a pleasant breakfast on the morning of the 12th.

When police tried to locate the janitor of the bank, Elwood Smith, he had apparently disappeared.

Miss Ellington stated that her brother Howard, when strolling to Taylor's Diner for coffee about 11:00 p.m. on Thursday, November 11, had seen Mr. Smith running from the bank.

Mr. Smith was found by the F.B.I. in Dogwalk, Georgia, on November 12. He had arrived there via Southern Airlines Flight 414 at 5:00 p.m. on the 11th.

The airline clerk confirmed the time of Smith's arrival.

Mr. Greenbags was the only person who had a key to the vault.

There were no planes out of Dogwalk between 4:00 p.m. and 7:00 a.m.

In addition to keeping payroll records, Mr. Ellington was in charge of the dynamite supplies of the Acme Construction Company.

Mr. Greenbag's half-brother, Arthur Nodough, had always been jealous of his brother.

Nodough always got drunk on Friday nights.

Arthur Nodough appeared in Chicago on Monday, November 8, waving a lot of money.

Arthur wanted to marry Camelia Smith.

Miss Ellington said that Smith had often flirted with her.

Mr. Smith's father, a gold prospector in Alaska, had died in September.

Mr. Greenbags waited in the terminal at O'Hare Field in Chicago for 16 hours because of engine trouble on the plane he was to take to Mexico City.

ANSWER: The *Ellingtons* collaborated to rob the bank, *Miss Ellington* supplying the front door key (borrowed from Mr. Greenbags) and *Howard* supplying the dynamite. Greenbags had already left for Brazil when the robbery took place. Mr. Smith was in Dogwalk on the night of the robbery. Dirsey Flowers was at the home of Anastasia's parents. The Ellingtons were lying when they tried to implicate Smith. There was no evidence that Arthur Nodough was connected with the robbery in any way.

The teacher can easily write clues for a mystery of his own creation, simply making sure that every clue is important. Some of the clues can serve as distractors, but these must be contradicted by other clues. The group might wish to attempt transferring their new skills to a subject-matter problem, one in which all students are in command of the basic information needed for solving it.

SKILL 4: TAKING RESPONSIBILITY TO CONTRIBUTE

In both the averaging-heights game and the mystery games it was necessary for all students to contribute, since each person had a piece of information essential to solving the problem. In these cases the students were told which piece of information they were to contribute (their height in the one game; the written clues they had been given in the others). And they were — hopefully — urged by others in the group to contribute their information so that the whole group might benefit.

The next step in discussion skills development is for the pieces of information to come from each student's own store of knowledge rather than being given to him. He must take responsibility for deciding what he wishes to contribute and when he wishes to contribute it. In the following activity every student must contribute at least once, and the sooner he contributes, the better the group's score will be. Subtle pressure is thus exerted on the timid members, and aggressive members are compelled to encourage the timid members to contribute.

Game

The group, seated in a circle with teacher outside, is given a question to discuss about which every student will know something from his own experience; for example, "How do teenagers spend their free time?" or "What is the best program on TV?" or "In what ways could our school be improved?" The rules are:

Every member must contribute.
Members must contribute in random order, not just in order around the circle.

The group that has followed the rules explicitly (every member contributing at least once in random order) in the shortest length of time is declared the winner.

Follow-Up

Observe the work of the group carefully. Note any changes over their performance on earlier problems. When they have finished, focus discussion on:

How did the group decide in what order students were going to speak?
Who kept order?
What means were used to encourage the more reluctant members to contribute?

Second Try

Give the students another question to discuss, similar to those suggested above. This time, instead of requiring every member to contribute within a certain time limit, give the group two points for each new person who contributes, one point for each subsequent contribution by the same person. By the end of the time limit, perhaps ten minutes, the group must come to some sort of conclusion and summarize it for the teacher. The group with the largest number of points wins.

SKILL 5: RESPONDING TO OTHER CONTRIBUTIONS

One of the most glaring weaknesses in a discussion carried on among unskilled participants is that rather than responding to what others are saying, participants add new, often unrelated ideas. This is not to say, of course, that fresh ideas are not needed in any discussion. However, students must become aware of what others are saying and react to those contributions, instead of simply tossing another new idea onto the heap. It is helpful for the teacher to point out that in a good discussion participants are doing more than just pooling their ideas — they try to combine their ideas into a group product. They build on the ideas of others rather than ignoring them.

This game demonstrates to students the type of interaction that results when members repond to one another. In a very artificial way students go through the motions of responding. Then, once they understand the nature of this type of interaction, they can return to a less structured format, free to choose whether to initiate an idea or respond to a previous one.

Game

Announce the question to be discussed, for example, "Should grades be eliminated?" or "Should a citizen ever disobey an unjust law?" or "Is the world of Orwell's *1984* better or worse than today's world?" Call on one student to give his opinion. When he has finished, ask another student to respond to speaker 1. He must look directly at speaker 1 and tell him in what ways he agrees or disagrees with his opinion. He may comment on or add to the previous opinion but he must *not* simply tell the group what his own opinion is. After speaker 2 has responded to speaker 1, ask another student to respond to speaker 2. He must look directly at speaker 2 and respond to his ideas. Continue until every group member has responded.

Follow-Up

Ask the group these questions:

Did you notice any times when a member ignored the previous contribution and presented a new idea?
What is the likely cause of failing to respond to previous ideas (not listening carefully, not trying to see relationships, and too concerned with one's own new idea)?

Second Try

Give every student a copy of a chart similar to the one below. Make any changes necessary for adapting it to the group such as a more appropriate topic, substituting actual names of class members, or expanding it to include contributions from all members.

Pattern of Interaction

Topic for Discussion: *Were the American colonies justified in revolting against the British?*

1. *Bill* starts discussion by giving his opinion.
2. *Tom* responds to *Bill*, indicating whether he agrees or disagrees and why.
3. *Debbie* responds to both *Bill* and *Tom* but gives no new idea. She simply states agreement or disagreement with *Bill/Tom*.
4. *Kevin* introduces new idea — his opinion.
5. *Ed* responds to *Kevin*.
6. *Charlie* asks *Ed* a question to clarify his opinion.
7. *Ed* answers.
8. *Tod* relates his opinion to that of either *Tom* or *Bill*.
9. *Tom* responds to *Tod*.
10. *Bill* responds to *Tod*.
11. *Larry* responds to *Tod*.
12. *Tod* replies.
13. *Charlie* presents his opinion.
14. *Erna* responds to *Charlie*.
15. *Hope* introduces new idea — her opinion.
16. *Mark* points out the relationship between *Hope's* opinion and those voiced by *Bill, Tom, Kevin,* and *Tod*.
17. *Dan* asks *Mark* what his opinion is.
18. *Mark* replies.
19. *Dan* responds to *Mark's* reply, revealing his own opinion.
20. *Luther* introduces new idea — his opinion.
21. *Ed* responds to *Luther's* opinion.
22. *Larry* responds to *Luther's* opinion.
23. *Erna* responds to *Luther's* opinion — indicates her view.
24. *Bill* summarizes the position of the group.

Instruct students to study the chart carefully, taking note of what type of contribution they are expected to make. Then signal "Bill" to begin. Students will probably have difficulty following the script smoothly the first time. Therefore, it might be helpful to give them a new topic and let them go through it a second time. When they have finished, they will probably have objections to such a highly artificial pattern of interaction. Explain that this exercise was merely a means of simulating a good discussion and that in an actual discussion they will be free to choose which type of response is most appropriate.

SKILL 6: CAREFUL LISTENING TO PERCEIVE DIFFERENCES

Often students, in their eagerness to trot out their own pet ideas, are not completely aware of the relationship between their idea and previous ideas. They may have discovered this problem when playing the games for Skill 5 above. A related difficulty seems to be the inability to perceive quickly the stand other members have taken on a topic. Students need to be able to summarize the position of all participants with a statement such as, "It appears, then, with the exception of a couple of us, that the group favors abolishing capital punishment."

The exercise explained below gives group members practice in perceiving and summarizing the differences between various opinions held by others. It is also helpful in sharpening their ability to state the issue.

Game

Announce a question or issue for discussion, for example "Can *Death of a Salesman* be classified as tragedy?" or "Are interracial marriages advisable?" or "Should girls share the cost of dates?" Appoint two students to present the two sides of the question. When they have finished, call on three students to summarize the differences between the two positions. The two students presenting the arguments judge the most accurate summary. Repeat with a new topic until all students have been called on to summarize.

Follow-Up

After each round of judging, ask students in what ways their summaries could have been more accurate. Try to identify the causes for their lack of accuracy.

Second Try

Substitute a subject-matter issue that students are currently studying, for example, the direction of the modern theater.

SKILL 7: CAREFUL LISTENING TO PERCEIVE AGREEMENT

Familiar to every teacher is the group of students who seem to equate discussion with argument and manage to turn every petty difference in opinion into a major altercation. They overlook the areas of agreement between members and fail to view these as important. These students need to understand the importance of finding areas of accord in discussion and to practice awareness of ways in which they agree with others.

The pattern of interaction required in the exercise below prevents students from disagreeing with another opinion until they have discovered all areas of agreement. It is a particularly useful device when used in conjunction with building responding skills (Skill 5).

Game

Announce the topic for discussion, preferably some issue on which the students will have strong opinions, for example, "Is mercy killing justifiable?" or "Should prostitution be legalized?" or "Is capitalism better than communism?" Appoint one student to state his opinion on the question. Then call on a second student to respond to the opinion of speaker 1. He must follow these rules:

First summarize the position of the speaker to demonstrate understanding of it.
Then state to what extent he agrees with it. Point out all areas of agreement but do *not* state any disagreement or arguments.

After the second student has responded to speaker 1, he then becomes the speaker. He states his opinion on the original question and points out any disagreement or arguments he was not allowed to state when responding to speaker 1. When he has finished stating his position, appoint a third student to respond to him, following the same procedure as above. Continue until all students have been both speaker and respondent.

Follow-Up

Discuss briefly the difficulties students had in following the instructions:

Why is it hard to state areas of agreement?
Why do we not usually bother to state agreement but hurry to disagree?
Why is it helpful to establish areas of agreement before disagreeing?

Second Try

Appoint four students to state their opinions on a controversial issue or subject-matter problem. A fifth student must then tell all points on which the four speakers agree or on which two or three agree. Continue until all students have practiced perceiving agreement. If the group is especially large, let them work together as the "fifth student."

SKILL 8: ENCOURAGING CONTRIBUTION RATHER THAN ARGUMENT

In their eagerness to show off their own knowledge or to beat others in an argument, most group members have a tendency to discourage the contributions of others rather than drawing them out. This problem was probably graphically demonstrated in the way the group attacked the mystery-game problem. Most persons seem to respond in ways that either "put down" the speaker and cause him to regret ever having opened his mouth or that engage him in a battle of wills, seeing who can win the argument. Students need to learn new ways of responding to other persons, ways that will encourage them to continuing talking rather than to withdraw.

The exercise explained below gives each group member a chance to practice new responses. His task is to draw out the other person and in doing so he can utilize any type of response so long as he does not argue.

Game

One group member chooses a topic to talk about, preferably something significant in his interpersonal relations. If the group is sufficiently unified and accepting of one another, a teacher might request that the topic deal with "a problem you do not generally like to talk about." If the group is still suspicious of one another, a less threatening topic will be necessary, perhaps a question such as "On what basis do you choose your friends?" or "What's your biggest problem at school?"

Before the speaker begins to discuss the problem or issue, appoint a member of the group whose role will be to listen in depth to the speaker and encourage him to keep talking. List on the blackboard and explain the various types of responses that help elicit contributions:

Raising questions ("When did you first begin to feel this way?")

Being supportive ("I have also felt that way, so I can sympathize with you.")

Clarifying ("Do you mean that your father frequently beat you or only threatened to?")

Reflecting what the speaker says or feels ("You apparently are very angry at your father for what he did.")

Giving examples from one's own experience ("A similar problem confronted me last year; my parents wouldn't let me use the car for dates.")

Remind the "listener" that he cannot under any circumstances take issue with the speaker. He must keep his own views out of the discussion and not try to prove the speaker wrong. Instruct the other group members to listen carefully to evaluate the effect of the listener's responses. They should note whether he ever argues and if he is successful in drawing out the speaker.

Follow-Up

Ask for a report from the observers. Ask the speaker how he felt about the listener's responses.

Second Try

Continue the activity until all members have been both speaker and listener, or let the group break into pairs and practice in-depth listening without the group observing.

SKILL 9: LEARNING NEW ROLES

In the previous activities students will have become aware of the different parts they can play in the on-going discussion process. They will have discovered as early as Skill 3, for example, how some group members apparently feel more comfortable than others in assuming leadership. They may have noticed that some leaders initiate only the procedural aspects of the discussion ("Okay, let's get down to work now. Who wants to go first?"), whereas others will assume a large part of the actual work ("I think that Mr. Jones did it, because of the blood in his hall.") At this point students need to be shown other roles that a member can play from time to time in the discussion process. They need to understand why these roles are important and when playing them is appropriate.

Game

Explain in some detail each of the following roles that a group member can assume at various times during a discussion:
Initiator
>Helps start discussion
>Organizes the group
>Introduces new ideas
>Raises new questions

Clarifier
>Asks for additional information
>Requests definition of vague terms
>Raises questions about previous contributions

Summarizer
>Brings group up to date on their progress
>Indicates where they stand on the issue
>Points out areas of agreement and disagreement

Evaluator
>Keeps group posted on how well they are attaining their goals
>Points out weaknesses in process

Then give the group a topic to discuss, either a controversial issue or a subject-matter problem. Distribute slips of paper, each of which indicates one of the following roles the recipient is to play:

Initiator
Clarifier
Summarizer
Evaluator
Observer (moves outside the group to watch)
Contributing Group Member

Instruct students not to tell anyone the role they have been assigned to play; they are to reveal it through their behavior during the discussion. After the discussion, the group tries to guess who was playing each of the roles.

Follow-Up

Discuss the ways in which these roles help the group to accomplish its goals. Ask for suggestions as to how the roles might be played more effectively. Let observers share their impressions of how the group worked.

Second Try

Repeat the procedure with a new topic and permit students to play different roles.

SKILL 10: ARRIVING AT CONSENSUS

Perhaps the most sophisticated yet most valuable skill that a group needs to develop is the ability to arrive at a group solution to a problem. Members need to feel that by working together they can produce a solution or conclusion that is superior to what they could accomplish working alone. They need to understand that compromising or changing one's opinion to further the group's goals is sometimes desirable. And they need to see that their individual contributions are important, not because they make one look good in the eyes of others but because they are essential building blocks in working out the group answer to a problem.

This skill was touched on in many of the previous games and exercises. It requires an attitude students have probably been aware of during the entire developmental sequence, but it is approached here in a more systematic way, to sharpen students' understanding of the process and to reinforce their previously developed skills. The game, perhaps the most complex one presented so far, requires students to use the best skills they possess for solving a problem. It will demonstrate to them the difference between results attainable by an individual and those attainable by a group. It will also encourage them to think through their own ideas when challenged by other members of the group.

Game

This "Lost on the Moon" game, devised by Jay Hall, associate professor of management, University of Texas School of Business Administration, is based on actual work performed by the National Aeronautics and Space Administration.

Distribute to each member of the group a copy of the following problem:

> You are in a space crew originally scheduled to rendezvous with a mother ship on the lighted surface of the moon. Mechanical difficulties, however, have forced your ship to crashland at a spot some 200 miles from the rendezvous point. The rough landing damaged much of the equipment aboard. Since survival depends on reaching the mother ship, the most critical items available must be chosen for the 200-mile trip. The fifteen items left intact after landing are listed below. Your task is to rank them in terms of their importance to your crew in its

attempt to reach the rendezvous point. Place number 1 by the most important item, number 2 by the second most important, and so on through the least important, number 15.

_____ Box of matches
_____ Food concentrates
_____ 50 feet of nylon rope
_____ Parachute silk
_____ Portable heating unit
_____ Two .45 caliber pistols
_____ One case dehydrated milk
_____ Two 100-pound tanks of oxygen
_____ Stellar map of the moon's constellation
_____ Life raft containing CO_2 bottles.
_____ Magnetic compass
_____ 5 gallons of water
_____ Signal flares
_____ First-aid kit containing injection needles
_____ Solar-powered FM receiver-transmitter

The game can be played in several different ways, depending on the amount of time the teacher wishes to devote to it or on what special needs the group has. The quickest, simplest use of the game is for the group to set to work immediately trying to arrive at consensus as to how the items should be ranked. Students should be reminded that their rankings must represent agreement by *all* members of the group and may not be arrived at by simply taking a majority vote. (A brief explanation of the concept of consensus, contrasting it to disagreement-reducing mechanisms such as vote taking, dictatorial rule, etc., might be helpful.) For this simpler use of the game, give the following instructions:

1. Read the problem explained on the distributed sheets.
2. Your task is to solve the problem as a group.

3. The only "catch" is that your answers must be agreed to by *every* member of the group. This will require that you spend a fairly long time talking over your ideas about each of the items and sharing any information you have that could help the group. While you should not be unduly stubborn, neither should you give in simply to speed the work of the group. Often one hard-headed member can save an entire group from making a serious error.
4. When you have made a final decision, record your group answer on a fresh copy of the problem and compare it to the answers prepared by the NASA.

Below are the correct rankings for the items, as determined by the space-survival unit of NASA:

15 Box of matches (little or no use on the moon)
4   Food concentrate (supply daily food required)
6   50 feet of nylon rope (useful in tying injured, help in climbing)
8   Parachute silk (shelter against sun's rays)
13 Portable heating unit (useful only if party landed on dark side)
11 Two .45 caliber pistols (self-propulsion devices could be made from them)
12 One case dehydrated milk (food, mixed with water for drinking)
1   Two 100-pound tanks of oxygen (fills respiration requirement)
3   Stellar map of the moon's constellation (one of principal means of finding directions)
9   Life raft (CO_2 bottles for self-propulsion across chasms, etc.)
14 Magnetic compass (probably no magnetized poles; thus, useless)
2   5 gallons of water (replenishes loss by sweating, etc.)
10 Signal flares (distress call within line of sight)

7 First-aid kit containing injection needles (oral pills or injection medicine valuable)

5 Solar-powered FM receiver-transmitter (distress signal transmitter, possible communication with mother ship)

Follow-Up

After the group has checked its answers against the ranking above, encourage them to evaluate their performance. Raise the usual questions about organizing, what roles different members played, and stumbling blocks encountered during the discussion. Then focus on the difficulties inherent in arriving at complete agreement:

> How did the group go about dealing with conflicts and disagreements?
> Which members felt they had to give in to group opinion?
> Was this good or bad?
> Would taking a vote on each item have been easier?
> Would it have been as effective?
> Why is vote-taking necessary?
> Is it always desirable?

Second Try

A more complex approach to this game, and perhaps a more valuable use of it, is to allow the individual members to rank the items *before* they join the group. The results of their working on their own can then be compared with the group results, and students can see the difference between the two. Using the game in this way might well require more than one class period; if the group works carefully, the game can be expected to take between one and one-half and two hours. For this more thorough use of the game, give the following instructions:

1. Read the problem explained on the distributed sheets.
2. Working entirely on your own, solve the problem by ranking the items in what seems to you to be the best order.

When students have finished, collect their papers and distribute fresh copies of the problem. Instruct students to form small groups of five to ten members, seated in a circle.

3. Now, try to arrive at a group solution to the problem. The group ranking must represent agreement by *all* members of the group and may not be arrived at by simply taking a majority vote. This will require that you spend a fairly long time talking over your ideas about each of the items and sharing any information you have that could help the group. While you should not be unduly stubborn, neither should you give in simply to speed the work of the group. Often one hard-headed member can save an entire group from making a serious error.

While the group is trying to arrive at consensus, the teacher can begin scoring their individual rankings:

1. Next to each item, jot down the difference between the student's ranking and the NASA ranking. For example, if the student has written 5 and NASA says 14, write down 9; or if the student says 7 and NASA says 2, write down 5.
2. Total the numbers you have jotted down. This is the individual score; the lower it is, the better the student's performance.
3. Average the individual scores to arrive at an indication of how the group did in general when working alone.

After the group has agreed to its ranking of the items, score the group results in the same way as the individual results. Then compare the group score with the average individual score. This will give an indication as to whether the group, working together, was more accurate than when working as individuals.

If the game is used with a large class divided into several smaller groups, it might be useful to score each group separately and make a chart comparing the results of the groups.

Follow-Up

Discuss the differences between the individual scores and the group scores:
  Why were they different?
  Did the group do better than all individuals?
  Does a group working together usually do better than most of its members working individually?
  Is this always true?
  Why or why not?
Next discuss the value of arriving at consensus rather than taking a vote:
  Would taking a vote on each item have been easier?
  Would it have been as effective?
  Why is vote taking necessary?
  Is it always desirable?
  How did the group go about resolving conflicts and disagreements?
  Which members gave in to group opinion?
  Should they have?

REMEDIAL EXERCISES

A DEVELOPMENTAL PROGRAM, such as the one suggested in chapter two, can be helpful in insuring that students have the essential skills for doing the discussion work expected of them in the classroom. However, every group will run into obstacles from time to time. Weaknesses in their skills will begin to show up as they engage in actual discussion situations. For this reason, it is useful for a teacher to have a basic repertoire of remedial activities designed to correct weaknesses as soon as they appear. To scold students when their discussion runs aground or merely to tell them how to do better is no substitute for giving them concrete practice in overcoming the problem.

The games and activities are arranged here according to the weakness they help correct. No sequence is implied. The teacher should familiarize himself with all the activities, so that he can use them without extensive preparation, or he can keep this book on file as a handbook, and refer to it for the appropriate remedy when his group begins to encounter difficulties.

Many teachers may wish to use some of the activities in this section to teach skills more advanced than those covered in the developmental sequence. Games from this section can be used to extend and enrich the basic sequence, but in general they should not be used until students have the essential skills developed by the basic sequence.

PROBLEM 1: OBTAINING FEEDBACK

Before a group can correct its weaknesses, it must become aware of them. It needs to know how it is doing and where its problems lie. Often simply knowing that a problem exists is all that a group needs to overcome it. This is particularly true with more intelligent and emotionally mature students. With other groups feedback may have to be accompanied by remedial exercises.

In working with discussion groups, one of a teacher's most important functions is to provide feedback. A teacher can view the work of a group objectively and base his observations on knowledge and previous experience that students may not have. A teacher should continuously watch the progress of the discussion and be ready to step in at any time to show the group how it is doing. Besides simple interruption by the teacher, there are other means of furnishing feedback to a group:

CONCENTRIC CIRCLES, sometimes called the "fishbowl" technique, allows some members of a group to observe and report on the work of others. The group is divided in half, with the working group seated in a circle inside the observing group. The observers can be instructed to look for general problems in the inner group's work, or they can be given certain special tasks. One student, for example, can be assigned to take note of students who look as if they would like to contribute but don't have a chance. Another could be assigned to spot which members dominate the discussion and which seem to be doing most of the actual work. Another could try to determine which helpful roles various members play during the course of the discussion. Students in the outer circle could also count the number of times their counterparts in the inner circle talk or keep a record of to whom their partner talks, revealing any particular coalitions that seem to have formed.

After the inner group has worked for fifteen to twenty minutes, the observers can report their findings and make suggestions for improving the quality of the discussion. Then, time permitting, the circles can exchange places, with the former observers now doing the discussing. After a period of time, the second group of observers can make their report.

A special use of concentric circles is to pair students with a partner in the other circle. The student in the outer circle watches the responses of only his partner and reports to him privately, making suggestions for improving his participation in the discussion. It is sometimes helpful for partners to work together over a long period of time to establish a trusting, and hence more helpful, relationship.

FREEZING THE ACTION interrupts the work of the group to allow it to talk over "How are we doing?" They should consider such questions as: "Are we attaining our goals?" "Are we working together in the most effective way?" and "Do all of us feel good about the way things are going?" In applying this technique, the teacher should guard against the temptation to tell the group how they are doing. It is essential that they themselves bring up their problems and devise ways of handling them. Freezing the action should take only a few minutes before the group resumes work. It is most effective if done briefly but frequently.

TAKE FIVE utilizes the last five minutes of the period, when the discussion is usually grinding to a halt anyway, for a quick evaluation of how the group worked together. Consider the same type of question as in freezing the action.

A QUESTIONNAIRE can elicit some important information about ways group members see each other and relate to one another. Do not require that students put their names on them and explain the need for complete honesty. Use mimeographed forms with such questions as:

> I like (or do not like) this group because . . .
> This group could function more effectively if . . .
> Which group member can most easily influence you to change your opinion?
> Which member can least easily influence you to change your opinion?
> Which group member do you have the most difficulty influencing to change his opinion?
> Which group member would you like to know better?
> Which group member do you feel is the best liked by the entire group?
> Which group member is most important to the success of the group?
> For me to be happier in this group, the other members should . . .
> Who in the group listens to you? Who does not?

The teacher can compile the results of the questionnaire and post them without fanfare on the wall of the classroom. Little or no discussion of the information revealed is necessary. The teacher must use discretion in revealing information that could be upsetting to a particular individual, for example, if one person was named by every other student as the reason they do not like the group.

ORAL QUESTIONING similar to that of the questionnaire is useful with a group that is well acquainted and comfortable with one another. It is generally best to raise one question at a time and go routinely around the circle, expecting each student to answer. This format exerts the subtle pressure necessary to prod students into overcoming their reluctance to deal with a threatening question. However, no student should be compelled to answer a question that makes him feel very uncomfortable. If he says, "I'd rather not answer" or otherwise indicates serious resistance, the teacher must accept this and move on. Nothing is accomplished by forcing groups to deal with problems that are overly threatening.

Nevertheless, it is usually very valuable for groups to go around the circle answering a question such as, "For me to be happier in this group, the other members should . . . " and it is generally possible to do this with minimum discomfort.

ROLE-PLAYING can be a useful device for showing other members how they are acting in the group. A teacher can give instructions such as the following: "For the next fifteen minutes I want you to continue your discussion as usual, except each of you is to pretend you are a different member of the group. You are to act exactly the way you have seen him act during a discussion. Mike, I want you to be Andy, and Andy, you be Mike. Toni, you be Alison; and Alison, you be Toni. Kevin, you be Ed; and Ed, you be Kevin," and so on until all students have been assigned a new identity. It is usually easier for students to remember whom they are playing and who is playing them if the assignments are made in matched pairs, but random assignments could be made.

Students might prefer to choose their own new identity and have the others guess who they were pretending to be. Besides providing students with feedback on how they appear to others, this game has the added benefit of giving students practice in understanding other members and seeing their point of view.

AN INTERACTION DIAGRAM can provide students with a graphic illustration of the way in which they are relating to one another, if most group members have overcome their defensiveness. Ask each member to write on a card the name of the one other group member who is "most important to the success of this group" or "with whose ideas you most nearly agree."

When all have finished, each person reads his response. The teacher or a group member draws a diagram on the blackboard, with circles representing each member, drawing arrows from the chooser to the chosen member. If care is taken to group the circles representing those members who tend to choose one another, a clear description of the group's pattern of interaction emerges. Care should be taken to phrase the question in a way not to cause distress, and the activity should not be utilized if members are still not comfortable with one another.

APPOINT AN OBSERVER to sit outside the group and evaluate its progress. If the observer is a student rather than the teacher, group members are probably more likely to accept his suggestions.

MECHANICAL MEANS of several sorts are available for furnishing a group feedback on its performance. Tape recorders can be used with little preparation, and as the recording is played back it can be stopped to allow for discussion of important aspects of the process. An increasing number of school districts are securing portable video-tape equipment. Although it requires some troublesome effort to set up the equipment and make sure lighting and sound arrangements are satisfactory, the resulting benefits to the group are well worth the added effort. The instant replay feature of video tape makes it the ideal means of showing a group what it looks like in action. Members can not only hear their responses but can see themselves and note their nonverbal behavior and how it affects the group. Like audio tape, a video recording can be stopped from time to time during the replay to allow for discussion of appropriate points.

PROBLEM 2: GROUP POLARIZED INTO WARRING FACTIONS

Particularly when a topic of discussion is a controversial one, groups often polarize into two or three factions, each taking an extreme position and refusing to compromise. The opposing faction quickly is perceived as the enemy and even listening to his point of view is treason. This problem frequently crops up with groups who mistakenly believe that the definition of a discussion is "heated argument." What is needed for these groups is some means whereby they can, first of all, realize that issues are not nearly as clear-cut as they may think and that one doesn't have to take an uncompromisingly extreme position to have an interesting discussion. These groups need to be given special opportunities to become better acquainted with each other to break down their image of opposing members as "enemies." They also need to be encouraged to see the issue from the point of view of the opposite side. Activites such as the following might be helpful:

A VALUES CONTINUUM can point out to the group that answers to questions are not always black and white and that we can and do often hold positions that are in the gray area between. For this game, the teacher should prepare a long sheet of butcher paper or shelf paper approximately seven feet long. Draw vertical lines to divide it into seven segments of equal size, and attach the chart to the blackboard at eye level. Label the extreme right end of the chart "Totally Bad" and the extreme left end "Totally Good." Explain to the students that the chart represents a values continuum (you may need to define continuum and give examples of other such scales, like thermometers, test scores, etc.). If an act were judged completely good, it would be placed at the far left side of the scale; if it were completely bad, at the far right side of the scale; and if it were judged somewhat in between these two points, it would be placed at the appropriate intermediate position on the scale. Tell the group that you are going to read to them a number of decisions. They are then to go up to the chart and indicate with a crayon or felt-tipped marker where they would place that decision as to its relative morality. A small circle with the member's initials inside is a good way to mark each position.

Describe for the group a wide range of decisions or acts, allowing time after each for every member to indicate his position. Possible situations might be:

> A high school senior writes a term paper for his girl friend, and she turns it in as though it were her own work. How would judge *his* and *her* act?

> A high school sophomore looks over the shoulder of a friend and copies four answers on a math test. How would you judge his act? How would you judge the act of his friend?

> A sixteen-year-old girl tries on several dresses and walks out of the store with one of them without paying for it. How would you judge her act?

An American soldier shoots a German soldier during World War II. How would you judge his act?

During World War II an American soldier, whose parents were immigrants from Germany, kills his Uncle Fritz who is serving as a captain in Hitler's army. How would you judge the American's act? How would you judge Uncle Fritz's decision to serve in Hitler's army?

Hitler orders the execution of six million Jews. How would you judge his act?

Commanders of the Allied Forces order the firebombing of Dresden, Germany, which resulted in the death of 135,000 civilians. How would you judge this act?

A teacher can devise another list of acts and decisions appropriate for his group. They should reflect a wide range of moral stances to allow for a great diversity of opinion. It might be useful but not necessary for the teacher to include some subject-matter issue of the type that the group has been discussing.

After all students have indicated their positions, the teacher can lead the group to interpret the results. Help them to see that although they may disagree violently on some issues, they are in close agreement on others. This device is particularly useful with groups whose members represent several definite identities: Protestants, Catholics, and Jews, or students, faculty, and administration, or various ethnic groups.

A SECRET SHARING DEVICE can create unity and improve members' ability to empathize, if the group's polarizing seems to be the result of weak group loyalty. For this exercise, members are given identical sheets of paper on which they are instructed to explain in detail some difficulty in their interpersonal relations that troubles them but which they would not feel comfortable sharing orally with the group. Urge them to camouflage their handwriting and not to allow anyone to watch as they describe their problem. Point out that it is important to explain the situation in detail, giving adequate examples and reasons. When everyone has finished, all the papers should be folded in the same way and collected. The teacher then shuffles them and distributes them in random order to group members. The members read the descriptions carefully, attempting to understand the problem as fully as possible and trying to imagine how the person who wrote the description feels about the problem. Then, proceeding in order around the circle, each student describes the problem he has read as though it were his own. He uses first person ("I...") and can change the description slightly to make it more appropriate to his own background, sex, and personal characteristics.

The important part of the process is that for the period any one is explaining the problem, he imagines himself to be the person who wrote about it. No discussion of the problems is necessary. Other students should not be allowed to ask questions, and no attempt should be made to guess who has each of the problems. After all members have presented the problems, the teacher can lead a discussion of their reactions with questions such as:

> How did you feel when you were writing down your problem?
> How did you feel when you explained the other person's problem?
> How did you feel when your problem was presented?
> Did the other person seem to understand your problem? Could he see it from your point of view?
> Do you feel you understood the other person's problem?
> How do you feel about the other members of this group?
> Have your feelings about them changed as a result of this activity?

The authors have discovered that when using this exercise the teacher can reduce students' anxiety by participating himself in the process. He should write a description of a problem along with the students and participate in the oral presentation of others' problems to demonstrate the procedure to the students and to set a serious tone for the activity.

INTRODUCING SOMEONE can help reduce conflicts. At the beginning of a period, assign each member to introduce someone on the opposing side. Each member must tell the group the other person's name and describe him to them, including interests, hobbies, personal characteristics, and the like. In making assignments, try to pair students who have been especially antagonistic or stubbornly opposed to each other.

CHANGING SIDES is another effective technique. Announce during a heated argument that for the next ten or fifteen minutes students are to change sides and argue the opposing point of view as vehemently as they have been supporting their own view.

ROLE-PLAYING, as outlined in problem 1, is a variation of the above. Assign students to pretend to be a member of the opposing faction.

PROBLEM 3: HOSTILE, OVERLY AGGRESSIVE GROUP

Somewhat similar to the group divided into warring camps is the group full of vociferous, often hostile, individuals who rarely listen to one another and fill the air with angry attacks on the contributions of others. The problem with these individuals is partly their unwillingness to listen (Problem 6) and partly the emotional outbursts with which they respond to other members. A healthy group can usually control one or two

such members, but if the entire group consists of this sort of person, remedies such as the following may be necessary.

CONTROLLED CONFLICT can clear the air of the noise and restore order. The teacher appoints one member to state in a single, clear sentence what his position is. The teacher asks those who disagree to raise their hands. The student who made the statement (speaker 1) chooses the challenger with whom he wishes to discuss the issue. The challenger states his objections to speaker 1's statement. Speaker 1 cannot interrupt him until he has finished. Then speaker 1 must attempt to understand his challenger's position as clearly as possible by asking questions and by restatement to check understanding. He must be able to restate the challenger's objection to the challenger's satisfaction before proceeding. Only then can speaker 1 defend his own position. He states his views without any interruption by the challenger. When he has finished, the challenger must clarify speaker 1's position in the same way speaker 1 did above and must restate it to speaker 1's satisfaction. The procedure is followed until the two participants or the teacher feels that the issue has been resolved or that greater appreciation of the other's point of view has been attained.

A MINUTE OF SILENCE between responses in a heated discussion can give participants an opportunity to reflect on the previous contribution and control their own emotions. The teacher should keep time, signaling to the group when to be quiet and when the sixty-second period is over and they can begin again. The time period can be adjusted to the needs of the group.

LISTENING IN DEPTH (Skill 8 in chapter two) will enable students to practice trying to understand another's point of view.

TO DE-EMPHASIZE DISAGREEMENT, require that the discussion take the form of the exercise outlined in Skill 7 in chapter two.

OBTAIN FEEDBACK, as suggested in Problem 1, by running a tape recorder during a particularly heated argument and playing it back for the group. Usually no discussion of the results is needed.

PROBLEM 4: THE SILENT GROUP

For most teachers the group that sits passively without any response is more frustrating than the noisy group. One or two quiet members can usually be dealt with successfully by other means (Problem 7), but if the group consists almost entirely of timid or apathetic students, it's hard to know what to do.

SIT IT OUT. Before the teacher panics, he should make sure that he has given the group adequate opportunity to respond before labeling them silent. Often a group will simply wait to see if the teacher really expects them to do the task or discuss the topic. In our anxiety, many of us fill the air with our own chatter and thereby affirm for students that we really didn't intend them to do the work after all. Our first suggestion, therefore, is simply sit it out. Assign the group a topic or a problem to solve (perhaps one of the mystery games in Skill 3, chapter two) and withdraw immediately, demonstrating that you intend for them to do all the work themselves. If their performance is being scored in terms of a time limit, they will soon start working.

NONVERBAL COMMUNICATION is a more radical approach that is sometimes helpful. Announce to the group that, because of some of the difficulties they have been having in verbal communication, you wish for them to practice nonverbal communication. Require that not a single word be spoken by any member for a period of, say, fifteen minutes. Since quiet members are usually comfortable only when others are talking, they will soon become rather ill at ease and will welcome the opportunity to begin communicating verbally. The period of enforced silence usually creates just enough anxiety to prod reluctant talkers into action.

PROBLEM 5: GROUP NOT WELL ACQUAINTED

Although getting to know one another should be the first thing that a group does, the process may require more than simply having members introduce themselves. The teacher may discover that members seem uncomfortable and suspicious of each other even after working together for several sessions. It may be necessary, therefore, for him to structure additional getting-acquainted activities.

DESCRIBING ONESELF to help others form first impressions has been outlined in Skill 1, chapter two.

THE INTERVIEW TECHNIQUE makes an interesting follow-up (see Second-Try under Skill 1, chapter two).

ANSWERING A QUESTION is another device. At the beginning of each period, students can go around a circle, reminding the group of their names and answering a question such as, "What is one thing that you like very much?" or "What do you dislike intensely?" or "What is your favorite rock group?" or "How do you feel at this very moment?" or "Who here are you most nearly like?" or "If you could be anywhere else but here, where would you choose to be?" or "What nickname would you give yourself right now?" None of the questions is particularly profound, but each gives other group members additional information about the person answering it. The authors have found it helpful to use a different question for each of the first five or six sessions of a group. By that time, students are generally familiar with each others' names and have begun to feel comfortable with one another.

INTRODUCING ANOTHER PERSON, outlined in Problem 2, is also a useful getting-acquainted device.

PROBLEM 6: IGNORING CONTRIBUTIONS OF OTHERS

Because of the eagerness we all have to show off our pet ideas and impress others with our extensive knowledge, we often use the periods when others are talking to formulate our next contribution. The result is familiar — rather than building on other ideas, we take the group into new areas or off the topic entirely. No group product results, and most members end up feeling as though nothing was accomplished. To help group members overcome this tendency, the teacher can utilize several activities:

MYSTERY GAMES, outlined in Skill 3, chapter two, demonstrate quite clearly what happens when contributions are ignored. They can be used to give practice in listening to and building on other contributions.

PERCEIVING DIFFERENCES activities outlined under Skill 7, chapter two, requires less time than the mystery games and can be used with subject-matter discussion topics.

SUMMARIZING what the previous speaker has said before adding their own contribution can be required of students.

PROBLEM 7: DEALING WITH PROBLEM MEMBERS

A group without one monopolist or silent member is indeed rare. The hostile member and the class clown exist almost as frequently. These familiar types often pose serious threats to the effectiveness of a group. Individual counseling or removal from the group is sometimes a solution, yet a healthy group can usually learn, we have found, to cope with these antigroup individuals and eventually incorporate the deviant members into the work of the group.

FEEDBACK is of central importance when a group has problem members. Often the problem member has little or no idea that he is acting inappropriately. If he has a chance to see on video tape or hear on audio tape his actual behavior and its effect on the group, he often will be motivated to change it without any further prodding by the group. Role-playing — pretending to be another member — is a particularly valuable way of letting other members show a problem member what he is doing (see Problem 1), but any of the other feedback devices can be utilized with success.

ROLE-PLAYING can also be used in a more general way to demonstrate the effects of anti-group behavior. This method is particularly helpful if the teacher does not feel it is advisable to point out the actual problem members with a feedback device. The teacher can explain to students the characteristics of each of the following anti-group roles: dominator-monopolist, hostile-aggressive member, silent member, and playboy-clown.

Then give the group a controversial issue or subject-matter problem to discuss. Distribute slips of paper, each of which indicates one of the following roles the recipient is to play in the discussion:

>Dominator-monopolist
>Hostile-aggressive member
>Silent member
>Playboy-clown
>Observer (moves outside the group to watch)
>Contributing group member

Instruct students not to show anyone the role they have been assigned to play but to reveal it through their behavior during the discussion. After the discussion, the group tries to guess who was playing each of the roles. As a variation, let the students decide themselves the roles they wish to play and see if the others can guess them.

PLAYING MORE CONSTRUCTIVE ROLES, such as an initiator, clarifier, summarizer, or evaluator, gives students practice in learning new skills. Use the activity described in Skill 9, chapter two.

FILL THE NEEDS of problem members in constructive ways. Most problem members are attempting, in the only way they know how, to secure the acceptance and recognition they so desperately need. Perhaps the most direct approach is to ask each group member to make a list of responses to the question, "What could members of this group do at this moment to make you happier?" After the lists have been compiled, students can take turns reading their lists, with the other group members responding to the needs as they are read. The information in the lists can also serve as data for guiding future behavior of the group toward problem members.

PROBLEMS PECULIAR TO THE SILENT MEMBER can sometimes be alleviated through use of an activity such as the one outlined under Skill 4, chapter two. This type of activity exerts just enough pressure on the silent member to prod him into sharing in the work of the group. Often once he has overcome his hesitancy, he will be able to push himself into contributing. In a class fairly evenly divided between monopolists and silent members — if such a painful circumstance can be imagined! — it may be helpful to assign the quiet members to the same small groups and likewise place all the noisy members together. In some cases, the loudmouths will solve their own problems once they discover that chaos results from their all trying to talk at once or they may need the help of the activities described in Problem 14 and Problem 3. When the silent members find themselves all assigned to the same group, they may be jarred into action. If they don't seem to respond, try the activities in Problem 4.

PROBLEM 8: STRAYING OFF THE TOPIC

One of the chief causes of a group's straying off the topic is poor listening (see Problem 6) or failure to build toward a group product (see Problem 11). Irrelevant ideas often result from members not keeping in mind what the group's goal is or how the present point relates to that goal. If this seems to be the group's problem, try the following exercise. Stop the action and ask a student to *state the issue* the group is supposed to be dealing with. Ask him also what the point under current discussion is and how it relates to the general goal. Such interruptions can be brief and should be made as frequently as necessary to keep group members aware of the direction in which the group should be moving.

PROBLEM 9: FIXED PATTERNS OF INTERACTION

When seated in a circle, members opposite one another tend to argue and ones seated next to one another tend to agree. This may be caused by the physical arrangement or by the fact that students usually sit beside people who like and support them. If feedback devices indicate that the group is forming certain coalitions, with the same group members talking to one another to the exclusion of others, it may be helpful to deliberately change seating arrangements. The teacher can work out a new seating plan and attempt to break up the fixed patterns, or he can make an announcement such as, "Notice carefully how you are seated today; tomorrow I want you to try to sit next to the person who is seated opposite you today," to encourage mixing. If the forming of coalitions seems to be the result of underlying hostility and suspicion, try using the activities outlined under Problem 2.

PROBLEM 10: THE INHIBITED GROUP

The inhibited group has the same symptoms as the silent group (see Problem 4), but its condition has been created by rigid, authoritarian control that has squelched free discussion in the past. Students may have had teachers who did not accept their contributions or who were critical of some of their ideas, or they may have been subjected to teachers who were so concerned with good posture and raising hands before speaking that students were afraid to be themselves and express themselves freely. To rehabilitate an inhibited group a teacher should first concern himself with creating a climate that encourages free response. He must accept students' ideas and withhold criticism, a difficult chore for those of us who feel obliged to point out the flaws in students' logic or the gaps in their knowledge. To create a noncritical atmosphere, a teacher may find it helpful to structure discussion activities that let students share their ideas without the threat of evaluation.

BRAINSTORMING is perhaps the easiest way to help a group overcome its inhibitions. In this familiar device, the group attempts to generate as many answers or solutions as possible without trying to sort out the good ones from the bad ones. The group is encouraged to work quickly and to refrain from commenting on previous contributions. This pattern of interaction differs, of course, from the one fostered by the activities outlined under Skill 5, chapter two, in which students are required to comment on and evaluate previous contributions. Brainstorming can be used with a general topic such as "How many uses for a brick can your group think of?" or with many subject-matter questions.

PROBLEM 11: TOSSING AROUND IDEAS RATHER THAN BUILDING GROUP PRODUCT

Once group members have overcome any inhibitions they may have had, they need to learn to stop simply generating ideas and start putting them together into a solution to a problem. This process requires careful listening to others (see Problem 6), commenting on previous contributions, adding to them, and evaluating them. For remedial work with this problem try the activities listed under Skills 3, 5, and 10, chapter two.

PROBLEM 12: ARGUING WITHOUT AGREED DEFINITION

The failure of many discussions can be traced directly to the group's lack of attention to definitions. Many times a group will plunge headlong into a problem or discussion topic without stopping to clarify any vague or ambiguous terms contained in the statement of the problem or issue. A group may find itself deadlocked because of its use of a word that may have several different interpretations, for example, "You can't call killing in war 'murder.'" In such cases, what a group needs is the ability to perceive the terms responsible for the difficulty — or those that may be potential troublemakers — and agree on a definition of these terms. The following activity is helpful in developing this skill.

AMBIGUOUS STATEMENTS which can either be discussion topics or statements made in the course of a discussion, can be presented to the group. For each they are to (1) locate any terms that may be vague, ambiguous, or controversial and (2) agree on a definition of these terms. The dictionary can be consulted only as a source of information and cannot be considered the final authority. Statements might be similar to these:

> Race riots are often the result of Communist agitation.
> Schools should teach only those subjects relevant to student's needs.
> Politicians are never good statesmen.
> Student demonstrations are harmful to our country.
> No good can come from a society that is not free.
> Draft dodgers deserve stiff prison sentences.

Subject-matter statements are also very appropriate for this exercise.

PROBLEM 13: ILLOGICAL REASONING

Helping students overcome errors in logic is no simple task. Many have been reasoning unsoundly since they first heard their parents mutter "Negroes are lazy bums." To deal with these weaknesses requires all the resources a teacher can muster, and it is beyond the scope of this volume to suggest the many ways a teacher can help develop sound logic. In general, pencil and paper exercises as part of the regular curriculum come as close as anything to remedying the problem. The exercises suggested here must be considered as an adjunct to a sequential problem developing reasoning skills.

Assuming that your group is continually over-generalizing, or attacking a person rather than his statement, or in some other way violating rules of logic, the following game can make them more alert to these violations in their discussion.

THE CHALLENGE GAME requires that the group be divided into two teams that will compete with each other for points. Explain briefly the three or four logical fallacies you wish the group to overcome. Your choice may be based on your observations of their previous discussions. Give the group an issue to debate, assigning one team to argue for it, the other against it. Instruct them to attempt to sneak into their arguments as many logical fallacies as possible, but they may commit only the fallacies you have explained in class. One way to score a point is to succeed in sneaking a fallacy past the opposing team. If the other team suspects a fallacy, any member of that group can issue a challenge. If the challenge proves correct, the challenging team scores a point.

PROBLEM 14: ALL TALKING AT ONCE

To help an overly eager group discipline and control its interactions, try: the mystery games outlined under Skill 3, chapter two, enforced periods of silence between contributions, as explained in Problem 3, or the consensus game suggested in Skill 10, chapter two.

PROBLEM 15: LOW TRUST LEVEL

No matter how skilled a group is in the mechanics of discussion, very little of significance will be accomplished if group members do not trust one another. The ideas they choose to share will be unimportant and insignificant if they do not feel they can put them before the group without fear of embarrassment, belittlement, or ridicule. But trust is not an easy thing to create in a group; it requires above all, working together over a long period of time. For this reason, the authors suggest keeping classroom groups together for no less than fifteen or twenty weeks. While trust building is a slow process, certain activities can be used to speed it.

THE GETTING ACQUAINTED activities of Problem 5 should be used extensively in the early stages of a group's work.

TEST TRUST by letting the group imagine how other members would react if they revealed an important secret. Each member thinks of some problem or fear that he normally does not talk about. He does not tell the group the secret but goes around the circle telling others how he thinks each person would respond if he *did* tell them his secret. He thus becomes conscious of how he perceives others, and they are provided with a sense of how trustworthy they are considered by others.

THE SECRET SHARING device is extremely valuable but cannot be used until students feel fairly comfortable with each other (see Problem 2). This activity can be repeated several times if the teacher desires.

THE FILL THEIR NEEDS device can help the group discern and supply the emotional needs of all the members (see Problem 6).

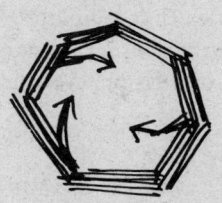

ON YOUR OWN

THE GAMES AND ACTIVITIES we have devised should be viewed by the teacher as only a beginning. Hopefully they will inspire him to create and adapt activities of his own to meet the needs of his particular groups. Our goal was not to compile an exhaustive collection of all the discussion activities available. We do hope to show fellow teachers that successful discussions are more than the fortuitous result of an interesting topic, that discussion skills must be taught to students and practiced by them, and that the most effective way to teach students these skills is through activities that simulate effective discussion.

For the teacher who wishes to investigate more thoroughly the problems of group discussion, we suggest the following:

Creative Discussion. Rupert L. Cortright and George L. Hinds. New York: Macmillan Company, 1959.

"Discussing as a Way of Learning" in *Teaching Adolescents in Secondary Schools.* Harry N. Rivlin. New York: Appleton-Century-Crofts, Inc., 1961.

Discussion and Conference. William M. Sattler and N. Edd Miller. Englewood Cliffs: Prentice-Hall, 1968.

Discussion, Conference, and Group Process. Halburt E. Gulley. New York: Holt, Rinehart and Winston, 1968.

The Dynamics of Discussion. Dean C. Barnlund and Franklyn S. Haiman. Boston: Houghton Mifflin, 1960.

Dynamics of Group Discussion. Dale Meredith Hall. Danville, Ill.: Interstate Printers and Publishers, Inc., 1964.

The Dynamics of Learning. Nathaniel Cantor. Buffalo: Foster & Steward, 1946.

Dynamics of Participative Groups. Jack R. Gibb, Grace N. Platts, and Lorraine F. Miller. 1951. $2.25; *Group Development.* Leland P. Bradford, editor. 1961. $2.; *Leadership In Action.* Gordon L. Lippitt, editor. 1961. $2. The above three titles are available from the NTL Institute for Applied Behavioral Science, 1201 Sixteenth Street, N.W., Washington, D.C. 20036.

Group-Centered Leadership. Thomas Gordon. Boston: Houghton Mifflin Company, 1955.

Group Discussion Processes. John W. Keltner. New York: Longmans, Green & Co., Inc. 1957.

"Group Life in the Classroom" in *Mental Hygiene in Teaching.* Fritz Redl and William W. Wattenberg. New York: Harcourt, Brace & World, 1959.

Group Problem-Solving Through Discussion. William S. Smith. Indianapolis: Bobbs-Merrill, 1963.

Group Thinking and Conference Leadership. William E. Utterback. New York: Holt, Rinehart and Winston, 1950.

Handbook of Group Discussion. Russell H. Wagner and Carrol C. Arnold. Boston: Houghton Mifflin Company, 1950.

How to Work with Groups. Audrey R. Trecker and B. Harleigh. New York: Woman's Press, 1952.

Learning through Discussion. Nathaniel Cantor. Buffalo: Human Relations for Industry, 1951.

Learning to Work in Groups. Matthew B. Miles. New York: Teachers College Press, 1959.

Now: The Human Dimension. Report of the Esalen-Ford Foundation Project in Humanistic Education. George I. Brown. 1968. Available from the Esalen Institute, Big Sur, California, 93920. $4.

Oral Decision-Making. Waldo W. Braden and Earnest Brandenburg. New York: Harper and Brothers, 1955.

The Structure and Dynamics of Change and Groups. Eric Berne. Philadelphia: Lippincott, 1963.

"Student-Centered Teaching" in *Client-Centered Therapy.* Carl R. Rogers. Boston: Houghton Mifflin Company, 1951.

Working with Groups. Walter M. Lifton. New York: John Wiley & Sons, 1961.

GENE STANFORD holds an A.B. in English from Washington University and a M.A. in Guidance and Counseling from the University of Colorado. He taught English at Horton Watkins High School in the St. Louis suburb of Ladue, Missouri, and is presently an NDEA Doctoral Fellow in Education at the University of Colorado. Mr. Stanford is the author of *Steps to Better Writing* in the "Aspects of English" series (Holt, Rinehart & Winston, 1972) and *McGraw-Hill Vocabulary 1/2/3/4/5/6* (McGraw-Hill, 1971), and is the editor of *Generation Rap* (Dell, 1971). He and Mrs. Stanford are coeditors of *Changes* and *Mix,* world literature anthologies in the "New World Issues" series, plus a companion composition program called *Journal 3/Journal 4* (Harcourt Brace Jovanovich, 1971). He has coauthored *Human Interaction in Education* (Allyn & Bacon, in press) and is a frequent contributor to educational journals.

BARBARA DODDS STANFORD holds an A.B. in English from the University of Illinois and an M.A. in the teaching of English from Columbia University. For six years she taught English at Vashon High School in St. Louis, Missouri, and is presently teaching English at Fairview High School, Boulder, Colorado. She is the author of *Negro Literature for High School Students* (National Council of Teachers of English, 1968), *I, Too, Sing America: Black Voices in American Literature* (Hayden, 1971), and *Myths and Modern Man* (Washington Square Press, 1972). With others Mrs. Stanford edited four volumes in the "Voices of Man" series (Addison-Wesley, 1970), and she is coauthor of *Theory and Practice in the Teaching of Literature by Afro-Americans* (National Council of Teachers of English, 1972). She has participated regularly in programs of the annual NCTE conventions and has written numerous articles for educational magazines.